Glory Days

James D. Wright

ISBN 979-8-89526-006-7 (paperback)
ISBN 979-8-89526-007-4 (digital)

Christian Faith Publishing
832 Park Avenue
Meadville, PA 16335
www.christianfaithpublishing.com

Printed in the United States of America

This book is dedicated to:

My best friend, Nick Biscan, who wanted to form a band with me, even as cancer was taking "his music" way too soon in life.

Mark Yuhas, friend and lead guitarist of the Jesters, who took his life, distraught over not finding "the music" again in his life.

My wife, Verlaine, for allowing me to carry on at least some of the "craziness" of "my music." Thanks for all the hours you spent typing and editing.

All those "garage bands" that "tried" regardless of their success.

Each and every musician in those old garage bands and all those generations of musicians since then.

Contents

Introduction..vii

1 Evolution 1

2 History in the Making 3

3 Life in the Balance 5

4 Vietnam Conflict 7

5 Gotta Have Soul, Angels, and a Savior 9

6 My Girl "Gloria" 12

7 My Favorite Garage Band...14

8 Michael Who?...16

9 War Is Hell 19

10 Duck Walk...34

11 My Kind of Town 37

12 One Hundred Sixty Miles of Gold 41

13 Through the Looking Glass 44

14 Rebirth 47

15 And Justice for All..50

16 A "Diamond" Opportunity..52

17 For God's Sake 55

18 Names and Numbers 57

19 More Name-Droppin' 60

Introduction

Four guys from Liverpool, England, would change music forever, and what a change it was. All over America, "garage bands" started popping up like mushrooms.

Guitar and drum sales went through the roof from a music epidemic proportion.

While there would be thousands of these garage bands, this author tells his story of being a pioneer and taking the lead to have "success" when others failed.

Why a book on garage bands, you ask? *Glory Days* is full of interesting true stories and experiences. That's why!

As you experience the "music" that has lasted over sixty years, you will see lots of "names" that you will surely know, like the Jacksons, Chicago, Buckinghams, and more. In some cases, Mr. Wright has a story to go with those "names." The author has changed the names of people or bands and, in some cases, has omitted them altogether, while some may have been enhanced for entertainment value.

The stories and content happen mainly in greater Chicagoland, but all over America—in fact, all over the world—garage bands were popping up. It would take volumes to put a dent in and do an individual tribute to each.

If you grew up in that time known as the sixties, then sit back, relax, and enjoy *Glory Days*.

1

Evolution

Ah, summertime! It was always a special time of year growing up on the southern shores of Lake Michigan in Indiana. The kids were out of school, the maple trees were in full foliage, and those annoying whirlybird seedpods were everywhere.

Yes, it was summer all right—the sandlot baseball games, the festivals, and neighbors catching up on the gossip from that long winter's grip.

There were those smells—ooh, those smells. Sometimes they weren't always pretty. The corn-processing plant, the soap factory, the oil refinery, and the steel mills all lend their special aroma, especially when the wind came out of the north over Lake Michigan.

For all the hustle and bustle of a city with a population of over one hundred thousand, the best part of summer was the sounds, or should I say lack of, but the summer of 1963 would change all that. Those days of street noises and the quiet of the early evening hours would never be the same again until years later.

What would this new sound be like? Only two school chums might have the answer to this one. My friend Willie and I would immortalize and entrench ourselves in a new sound. After only two months, by April, we knew what that new sound had to be—it had to be four guys with guitars and drums, and vocals too! Yes, a rock and roll band, not with horns, not with doo-wop street singers, but an actual amplified sound with a drummer!

I said April would make a difference, and it would—it would probably change my life forever. You see, Willie had just received an English music catalog from "across the pond," and it was stocked with songs by groups with names like the Troggs, Moody Blues, Rolling Stones, Dave Clark, the Zombies, and the band that would in less than a year change the history of music—the Beatles.

We started buying these Beatles records from England. I can remember the first Beatles song we learned was "That Boy." It was followed by "Till There Was You," "Please Please Me," "Twist and Shout," "I Saw Her Standing There," and "Chains."

Summer would pass, but the band got tighter. That summer, the neighborhood girls would come down to watch, and the guys would stop by to hang out and get their fill of "cool quotient."

We practiced at my house most of the time. I guess my parents tolerated the noise—I mean music—in those early months. It was better to know we were in the garage or the basement than getting in trouble or sharing this experience with the other band members' parents and their neighbors. Why share when they were getting the "whole experience"? There was even a side benefit from the bass drum—it kept my parents' hearts regular.

By Thanksgiving, one thing was obvious—the British were coming, the British were coming for the New Year.

2

History in the Making

Sunday nights are usually TV nights. My mom, dad, and even our cat, Tiger, would watch television together. Tiger just loved *Lassie* on TV. When the boy called for Lassie at the beginning of the show, Tiger would come running from wherever he was in the house. Sometimes, he'd stick around to see if *The Wonderful World of Color* offered anything he might want to watch.

I was setting up my monaural tape recorder because tonight I was taping the forerunner of the British Invasion the Beatles. It was going to be a history-making night, maybe a world-changing event.

The Wonderful World of Color had ended, and Tiger had given a final check on my recording equipment. Normally, Tiger would be off to a cushy, quiet, probably dark room or corner by now. No, sir, Tiger wanted to see those mop tops. He seemed to dig the meew-sic, if you know what I mean. Just as my dad didn't care for the screaming girls, I don't think Tiger did, either! Watch out, Topo Gigio and Mary Martin—tonight would belong to the Beatles and their screaming fans.

The *Ed Sullivan Show* would get a 70 percent TV rating market share. That was an all-time record that only a show called *American Idol* could even come close sixty years later.

My band, on the other hand, was not on TV; however, we were getting more and more gigs to play. We even recorded on an old studio recording machine. How cool! A friend of ours brought over this heavy monster of a recording device to my home. All this sounds really cool, except we recorded it in my dad's garage. The recording device was extremely hot, and not only did it record, but it also made a finished 78 rpm record. The records were of poor quality, and we made three of them. I never knew what happened to them, but I suspect.

Just as things were popping, we would have to find a new drummer, and Willie and I would split for creative differences. Luckily, we found a lead guitarist named JJ. He and I would ultimately take different paths, but we have remained friends to this day.

JJ and I played in a couple of different bands. He played lead and could sing lead, giving me a break as I had been singing quite a bit before he joined us.

I mentioned we had to replace our drummer. We would go through a couple of drummers during the next year.

We made it through that summer playing some Beach Boys tunes and at least a song by all of the British Invasion bands. If a song was on the Top 40 list, we learned it.

3

Life in the Balance

The music was better, the jobs got better, and we were making money. Life was fun!

While playing a performance one night, we met a booking agent whose office was in Chicago. Mark was a Jewish agent with whom I would remain in contact for several years. He and I struck up a friendship that I would never forget.

Of course, he wanted to sign our band—that was his job—but other than that, he appreciated "good" talent. We never did sign with him, but that was okay. He would provide some great opportunities over the next few years.

The band would have a name change and a new look. We all would get matching red tuxedo dinner jackets, black pants, gray high-top boots, and a tricornered hat.

We still continued doing Top 40 songs despite the suits, on into another year. JJ and I knew the band probably wouldn't see the New Year out, and we would be right.

The Vietnam War was escalating at a rapid rate. We would watch the local news just to find the inevitable "body count" on each broadcast.

The year 1965 was fun while it lasted; we played a lot. We got better and better jobs, and our friend Mark was ever finding us work for 5 percent to 10 percent a job.

In the late spring of that year, I sojourned over on my Ward's motor scooter to pick up our other guitarist. Boll Weevil, as we nicknamed him, could play anything.

That particular day, we would run into a heavy rainstorm on our way to Swede's house. Swede was our drummer and the oldest member. As we rode through the rain, it got darker and heavier, and all of a sudden, it got light and sunny, and we could see blue skies. A split second later, it was much like it was before—gloomy, dark, and we were soaked.

When we arrived at Swede's, his mother was in the doorway, as we must have been a sight for sore eyes! Here we were, Boll Weevil, long and tall, and I, at 150 pounds, riding soaking wet on my moped! His mother told us that a tornado had just gone through the park we had just passed by and caused major damage to the roof of a big variety chain store.

It was then we realized what really had just happened. The storm, it seemed, was hopping all around, and the "blue sky" we noticed had to be the tornado going over the top of us. If it had taken to the ground, we would have been swept up in the fury.

That would be the first of several situations in which I was glad God was with me.

Boll and I looked at each other, and you could see fright in each other's eyes, yet relief from what could have happened. We never talked about it again.

4

Vietnam Conflict

The summer of 1965 meant more kids in the neighborhood were playing guitars and drums. Of "noteworthiness" (pardon the pun) were two teenage girls, both my age.

Dee was the more experienced, quick-learner type. At the time she was available to play, our band was still together. Mo was the second girl and could play a fair guitar.

As Mo and Dee were both good-looking girls who could play guitar, what more could a band ask for?

Dee would go on to play with some other neighborhood kids. On the other hand, Mo would continue practicing every day. I could hear her practicing from my house.

The summer shows started to pick up, and so did the Army call-up list for a free vacation to Vietnam. It would also be the first call to take our drummer, Swede, and our guitarist, Boll.

JJ and I were right. We didn't see the end of 1965; in fact, we just made our summer obligations that year.

I started dating an Italian girl that summer. I can remember she had a backyard party for her birthday, and JJ and I showed up with our instruments. We were told there would be a guy at the party who could play drums, so I brought my set with everything else.

We made our final sound check and began playing. Just a few notes into the first song, we were under the realization that the drummer did not know how to play. We graciously got through the first song before ushering the drummer wannabe off the stage. JJ and I would finish out the party with him on guitar and me on the drums.

JJ knew of a drummer who lived a few streets over from him. He was a Jewish kid and could drum fairly well, had equipment, and had a good attitude.

We played for a short time, but it just wasn't what we had before. JJ and I knew that the time had come to say our first goodbye.

I had been taking some work for some time that Mark (the agent) had sent my way. I was playing in a house band that opened for big names that came through the Chicagoland area.

Fortunately, this experience would last for a few years more. I will devote a chapter later on with some of those experiences.

The summer of 1965 also brought me a chance to see—not hear—the Beatles at Chicago White Sox Comisky Park. With an entourage of security, the boys came in via a golf cart from center field to where the bandstand was set up at second base.

For two hours, the girls' screams would go back and forth from loud to louder. For one brief moment, the screaming stopped, and I heard two words, "I'm Down," which apparently was the hit that they were currently singing before the screaming began once more.

I was there with my neighborhood friend Warny. He, too, shared my passion for the Beatles. This was huge for us; otherwise, we'd be playing baseball or playing with our collection of Tonka and Structo trucks.

Both of us left Sox Park, knowing we witnessed history in the making; we just didn't hear it. Warny would go on to play in a garage band doing Led Zepplin.

The year 1966 would find Willie, the former lead guitarist, and me in the dean's office. It wasn't because we were bad; in fact, it was to be able to have special permission to occasionally miss school so our bands could perform as needed. We also were allowed to grow our hair a little longer than usually accepted. Teddy was the dean, and he stood about five feet tall and had one of those horse laughs. Teddy would check our hair, check our schedules, and check our grades. Willie and I would barely pass all three criteria, but it was worth it to see Teddy and hear him laugh.

5

Gotta Have Soul, Angels, and a Savior

I picked up the telephone, and JJ was calling about a job in a band he and a drummer had. It seems their band had certain members getting all-expense-paid vacations to Vietnam too! They were looking for a bassist and a rhythm guitarist.

I told JJ about Mo, and with a little encouragement from us, Mo agreed to be in her first band. She was ready, and her practicing paid off.

Mo and JJ both played lead and rhythm guitars. Mo looked good, played well, and added a new dimension to the group. The band continued for a few months up to the holidays. We broke up after the drummer's mother owned a nightclub and stiffed us out of our money. We were angry we had just been taken by our drummer's mother, of all people.

As I recall, a couple of fluorescent signs weren't working when we left. I have no idea what happened to them!

This would be the last time JJ would be seen onstage with me until forty-eight years later. JJ and I had been good friends, and we were drifting apart. He started hanging out with some guys I knew, and they started experimenting with drugs. This only drove a bigger wedge between us.

I had started doing a lot of acoustic guitar work, mainly solo. I finished out the year playing various folk clubs around the tristate area.

The year 1966 came in much as 1965 went out. I was taking solo work in folk clubs, and Mark was still getting me electric bass gigs opening for the stars. Even though the year started slowly, I would wind up in two of my favorite bands ever!

I got a call from a band on the north end of town. Four of the guys went to the local Catholic high school, and one went to the same public high school as I did.

The band played blue-eyed soul music and had two lead singers who could sing like any male or female soul (Motown) artists of the day. It was fun music and had a beat, love songs with quality lyrics; and we were one of only a few bands that played this music.

Even though great soul artists such as Brook Benton, Sam and Dave, Temptations, Four Tops, Wilson Picket, and Otis Redding were selling records, there still was that color barrier. White stations were starting to play black music, and as the popularity grew in the mid-'60s, more and more stations would put them in their Top 40 format.

Our little soul band started to grow by leaps and bounds. We even got a call from a West Coast lawyer saying he had a client with a domain on the name of our band. The group was a black soul group that had been around for years and even had some 45 releases and an album or two. We dropped the word *Soul* in our name, and we were good to go!

There were several memorable moments with these guys. I can recall playing for a Latino wedding when, after an hour or so of playing and everyone "grooving" to our music with a couple of drinks, the best man called for a grand march—a grand march! We didn't have a grand march—we were a soul band! What made matters worse was that our rhythm guitarist, Bird, and Ski, one of our lead singers, left to join the grand march. Just as our lead player was starting to panic, our drummer started playing a beat on his drums, and Mitch, our other lead singer, started singing "When the Saints Go Marching

In." In just seconds, I figured out the chord pattern and showed our lead player, Luke. We all came together, and a grand march was born!

We were playing with tears in our eyes from laughing so hard. Twenty-seven minutes later, the grand march came to an end. Needless to say, we were all over Bird and Ski when they rejoined us for leaving us in the lurch.

Bird was also a member of the Chicago sector of the Hell's Angels Motorcycle Club. The Hell's Angels of California were getting a lot of press in the mid- to late '60s for their criminal and dastardly antics.

The Chicago sector, however, were bike riders. The ones I met were friendly, helpful, and passionate about riding Harleys.

Bird was a friend, not just a band member—he could boogaloo for a big (I mean *big*) man.

At some point, the Angels became our roadies and would escort us to our gigs.

I'll never forget the look on the Father's and Mother Superior's faces as we "tooled" up to a Battle of the Bands competition at the local Catholic high school with our Hell's Angels entourage.

I don't know how many "Our Fathers" and "Hail Mary's" were most likely brought upon the four Catholic members of our band, but whatever happened, it diverted disaster. The Father and Mother Superior almost didn't let us play due to our illustrious escort service.

Dan was the bassist for one of the competition bands that day. It was good he was there and was a friend because I broke a string on my bass and didn't have a replacement.

Dan offered the use of his bass, and thus we finished our segment without any further problems.

Dan and I were constantly in the local papers and their polls as the top two bassists from Northwest Indiana. Other than Nick Fortuna from the Buckinghams, Dan and I also got kudos from Chicagoland newspapers as two of the top five bassists.

Things were good—real good. However, by midsummer, all but the drummer and I would get a free vacation to Vietnam. Uncle Sam was passing out a lot of those all-expense-paid trips to the Asian rice paddies.

6

My Girl "Gloria"

Being in a band made dating easier; however, I was starting my second year with my Italian girlfriend, Donna.

Her sister thought I was cool because I was a musician and I had a moped.

Donna's mother, on the other hand, would have liked me better if I was Catholic. I would remind her that I would like her even more if she didn't remind me of what religion I wasn't affiliated with.

There was another girl in my life, and I had had a relationship with her since October of 1963. Her name was Gloria, and actually, "she" was a song ("Brown Eyed Girl") written by Van Morrison.

Morrison was in a band called Them and had a song called "Baby Please Don't Go." The flip side was "Gloria." The song, as done by them, was choppy and murky at best. I showed Willie the song and how I "cleaned" it up. He agreed with what I did with it, and he "cleaned" his lead guitar part. It was a hit. Every time I play it, even today, the crowd loves it!

Fast-forward to October of 1965. JJ, Mo, and our drummer were playing for my high school drama club dance. "Gloria" was a song that JJ and I would have a history with for over a year and a half.

At the dance that night was a senior classmate and at least one member of his band. The band was based out of a southwest suburb of Chicago. Remember, this was October 1965.

In June of 1966, roadie and friend AJ called me at about 10:30 p.m. one school night and was all over me because we didn't tell him we released "Gloria." He said he had heard it on the top rock station in Chicago. I assured him it wasn't us.

The next morning, on the way to school, there it was—my girl "Gloria" on the radio. If it wasn't that we didn't record it, I could swear it was us too! The style, guitar licks, timing—all was just as I had been doing it for almost three years.

Over thirty-five years later, I would meet a fellow at a Chicago record convention. He was into "garage bands" and local Chicago music history. I told him of my relationship with "Gloria" and how it "seemed" interesting that the band that went on to record the song was at that school dance that past October.

Sometime later, the fellow I met at the record show emailed me that he had run into two of the members of that group and told them of my story. He said the members of the band graciously would not "confirm or deny" my story.

One thing about those high school days—it seemed like someone was always trying to take your girl.

7

My Favorite Garage Band

As I previously mentioned, Uncle Sam "souled out" our band, and once again, my time in the musician's unemployment line would be short-lived.

Only a couple of months earlier, I read a piece in our local newspaper about two brothers who had a band; one played bass and the other guitar. Funny it seems that shortly after the article came out, they had won an all-expense-paid trip to Vietnam.

I suppose I should have looked in the Vietnam want ads for musicians as they seemed to be all over there!

I got a call to play bass for a band called the Jesters. That was the same name of the brothers' band I had read about in the newspaper.

The drummer, Ray, called me and said my buddies at the local music store gave him my name. Ray asked me to come down to audition. The rest was history, and I was given the job after the first song. I knew their playlist, I could sing lead and background vocals, and they were getting an award-winning bassist.

Up to this point, I have purposely avoided mentioning names of former groups, but the Jesters were magic. We had Tony on lead vocals, Bruno on keyboards, Ray on drums, and Mark on lead guitar. We were a Top 40 band and kept up with all the latest hits.

These guys would work, they learned, and that made them good—no, very good—at their craft.

Bruno could make his Farfisa chord organ do anything. Ray hadn't played drums long but learned to play well. Tony could sing with the best of them, except he would work so hard that I would usually take over on lead vocals halfway through the third set because he would lose his voice. Mark was most happy when playing in the band. He could learn and improvise leads with the best of them.

We got a job doing sock hops at a local high school every other week. The week we weren't there, another group was. There was an all-girl group, the Riots; and as time progressed, it would become our opening act at other multiple band venues. The girls were very good, and we were friends with them.

We got more and more work, and we would breeze out of 1966 as one of the best area bands of 1966. The girls would finish number 2 that year behind an all-girl band from Gary, Indiana, the Powder Puffs.

Mark, my agent friend, liked the Jesters and was devastated when the "soul band" broke up. He helped us get work, and once again, the jobs got better, and we were seeing, doing, and meeting people and playing venues that previously we would never have had access to.

Some of these people and events will be detailed in further chapters. Like the next one!

8

Michael Who?

After nearly two years, my Italian girlfriend, Donna, and I would go our separate ways. We had grown apart, and I was just too involved with my real life, music. I bet her mother was very relieved.

My work with Mark, the agent, had brought me chances to work with groups like the Animals, Turtles, Tommy James and the Shondells, We Five, the Hollies, Steve Goodman, and Blues Magoos, just to name a few.

Little did the Jesters know we would make history and see history in the making that year, not once but three times.

The first time was a battle of the bands competition in Gary, Indiana. A black group of brothers from Gary were among the sixteen bands who entered the competition. They called themselves the Jacksons. The battle of the bands was being held in Gary and promoted by a Gary radio station. Needless to say, the "white" bands from Gary took the top spots. At position number 2 was—you guessed it—the Jesters. The Jacksons went on to be thirteenth or fourteenth on the standings list. Not to take away from Gary's talent, but only two of their bands should have been in the competition.

Just a few months later, another band competition with just eight bands would take place. We finished second in that one, and if I recall correctly, the Jacksons finished dead last.

A local disc jockey from Chicago would host teen dances four nights a week. Thursday nights would be just southwest of Chicago.

Friday nights occurred in Hammond, Indiana, about a mile and a half from where I grew up. Saturdays were always in a far southwestern town fifty miles from downtown Chicago. Back to Indiana on Sundays, about twelve miles south, would be the fourth and last of the locations.

The dances would have a very unique format: It would have two bands that would play two forty-five-minute sets each. The first band up would most likely be a local Chicago area band. Most times, the first band would be a one-hit wonder or a popular local band without a record.

On a particular Friday night at the Hammond location, we showed up early, as we had done before, so we could get our equipment set up. Our DJ boss wasn't there that night, but Chuck, his right-hand man, was present.

I asked Chuck, "Who are we opening for?"

Chuck replied, "Some band from Gary. The Johnsons or something like that."

He could no longer get the last word out of his mouth when a big black man came through the door asking for the person in charge.

The second person who walked through the door was a guy I had homeroom with in the mornings at school.

I asked him, "What are you doing here?"

He went on to explain that he was in his "cousin's" band and that he was the keyboard player for the group.

Chuck didn't tell us then that the Jacksons were opening for us!

It was rough to see the Jacksons perform. They were doing Top 40 rock 'n' roll, which had been predominately white music nationwide. Somehow, seeing songs like "Hang on Sloopy" and "Louie, Louie" from them weren't cutting it. The crowd started booing, and that made it even worse. They hung in that first set after almost leaving after the fifth song. I give Papa Jackson and the boys kudos for bravery under fire.

We started playing, and our song selections, style, and abilities only added to the Jacksons' discomfort. They did come back for their second set, much to the crowd's disdain, finished the set, grabbed their equipment, and left almost before we finished our first song.

Six months later, the Jacksons would be playing for a gala event in Gary, and it was rumored that Diana Ross was in attendance. The rest would be history.

9

War Is Hell

The holidays were coming, and we were, for a brief moment, looking to the band's future. While the Jacksons' future was a little over three months away, ours was bright and promising.

Our thoughts were on the Big Time and recording. We were ready, excited. At our next practice, we were going to make plans for the band's future. I couldn't wait to get to practice that week. The expectation of our future was mind-boggling.

Then it happened. Tony and Bruno had just gotten their travel vouchers from Uncle Sam. Silence, tears, anger, frustration—all ensued after they spoke those words that I had heard relentlessly: "Going to 'Nam."

God knows I hated that war! I was tired of watching it on the six and ten o'clock news; I was tired of the body counts, the inhumanity; and I was tired of good musicians and friends getting one-way tickets to a rice paddy.

Ray, Mark, and I at least had a core we could rebuild from, and we tried. We tried out numerous musicians, to no avail. It wasn't the same.

Just as we were adjusting that it wasn't the days of old, the worst happened. Mark got his official "greetings" letter three months later. It was January or February of 1968, and he was gone.

Ray and I would try for a couple of months to restructure the band, with no success. Ray and I parted in defeat. He would drum for another group, and I would step up my solo folk music career.

A girl whom I went to high school with was doing the folk club circuit too. One night, when I had a rare Saturday night off, she invited me to catch her act. So I went down to a club just a couple of blocks from my house where she was playing. She was awkward onstage with her nervousness, and her guitar skills were limited. I managed to clap, cheer, and yell "groovy"—whatever it needed to arouse the almost lifeless crowd. Nothing seemed to work. The crowd was eating, on drugs, or distracted. One of the couples was oblivious to everyone as the guy was doing rather well copping a feel from his girlfriend's chest. Another couple was flat stoned from doobie, getting karma from just being "in time."

If all this wasn't enough, Joanie asked me to come up and sing with her. We did Peter, Paul and Mary's "Leaving on a Jet Plane" by John Denver. We did one or two more together, and then it happened. She walked up to the microphone and announced that she was taking a break but that I would continue performing. She handed me her guitar, and I played a Byrds song, a Woody Guthrie song, and others. The crowd became more responsive, and when it was the end of my last song, shouts from the audience to "keep playing" emerged.

The manager begged me to keep playing that night, and I politely declined.

Joanie would go on to do a few more songs to finish up what would be her last night at the club.

As I was leaving, the manager stopped me and offered me a playing gig at the coffeehouse. After a lot of persistence on the manager's part, I eventually took a rotation playing there.

I would see Joanie one more time a few months later at graduation. She said she was mad because I transferred high schools in my senior year. She didn't know the manager had offered me a job that night at the club. I often wonder if she really was upset about something else—hmm.

Practice makes perfect.

Here I am at the Burrito Bandito Restaurant in Portage, Indiana.
I'd perform all types of music, and I would write songs about
the local politicians, which patrons would come to enjoy.

Marquette Park was the place to be in the summer, right on beautiful Lake Michigan. Sandy beaches and live music filled the air. I always liked playing there. Oscar and the Majestics were from Gary, Indiana, which Miller was a part of. Oscar was an eccentric. For example, the guitars had a shield that was strapped to the neck of the guitar with the band name on it. I was told by a band member that Oscar did not want people to know what chords they were playing! Trust me, they played no originals at that time, so who cared what key they were playing in?

This poster shows what a typical star lineup could be—
lots of talent and usually three to five acts a show.

The Impacts lasted about as long as it took to get started. At left
is me on bass; center is Maureen Leahy, second lead guitar; and
right is John James on first lead guitar. Rick is on drums.

Little Boy Blues from the Chicago, Illinois, area played very good blues. "I'm Ready" was the only record I know that got airtime on Chicago radio stations.

Playing with my favorite group, the Jesters,
October 1967 on my Framus bass.

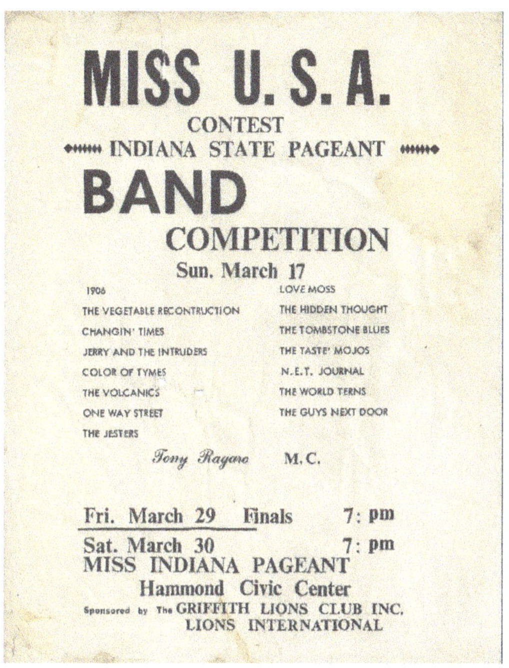

The Jesters was my favorite band of all time—
maybe because I was the bass guitarist!

Bill Hansen was the lead guitarist and group leader for
the Jordans. Bill and I originally played together some in
1963. The Jordans would later become the Takers.

The Panel, from Chesterton, Indiana (Porter County), area. The best teenage band I ever heard.

Saturday's Children were five fantastic musicians who could sing as well as they played. They had great stage presence and original songs; my all-time favorite band from Munster, Indiana. They had two 45 releases on the Chicago charts, yet their record label did nothing to promote them. Kudos to a great band that sadly became another pop tragedy.

For several years, I scheduled the entertainment
and participated in a local Indiana festival.

The *Hullabaloo* was a nationally televised dance/pop music show in
the mid-1960s. The one pictured above was one of several franchised
clubs across the country. This club was located in Portage, Indiana.

L to R: Scott Conner, dulcimer; Richard "Thurman" White, banjo; Jim Wright, acoustic guitar. Scott is the best dulcimer player and manufacturer that you will ever find. Thurman is dynamite on the banjo and four other instruments.

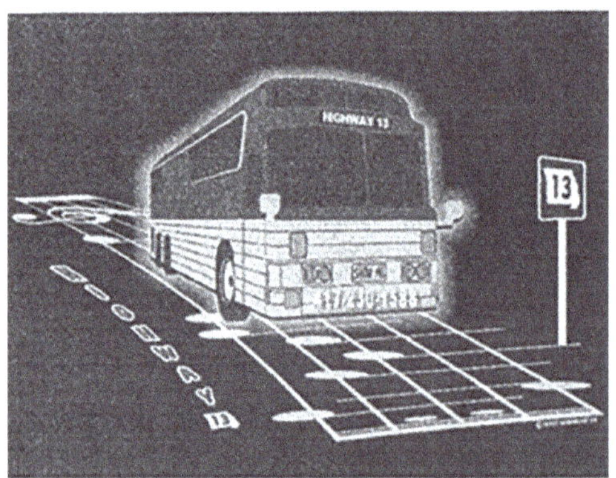

HIGHWAY 13 BAND

APPEARING
9 PM SATURDAY FEBRUARY 16, 2008

AHOY'S

KIMBERLING INN RESORT
6 PIECE BAND PERFORMING A VARIETY OF: Country, 60's, 70's, Pop, Rock-N-Roll, and other favorites.

DINNER SPECIALS

I was the original bass player for Highway 13 Band. The bus pictured was an original tour bus for Motown's "Temptations."

LIVE MUSIC SCHEDULE

May 11	Highway 13
May 25	Brenda Meyer Band
June 1	Madison Avenue
June 8	The Fury
June 15	Third Degree
June 22	Shawn Campbell, Katie Linson and the Band Rescue
June 29	Sugar Creek Blues
July 4	Kimberly Patrick
July 13	Jim Wright 50th Anniversary Band
July 20	Smooth Down Under
July 27	Smokin' Joliet Dave & the Mighty Mudhounds
Aug 3	Highway 13
Aug 10	Kickin' Kountry
Aug 17	Brenda Meyer Band
Aug 24	Sean Clavin & the Dirty Truth
Aug 31	The Fury
Sept 14	Kimberly Patrick
Sept 28	Crash Landing
Oct 12	Highway 13
Oct 26	Madison Avenue

Baxter, Missouri: I put together a band to celebrate my fifty years in music.

Good food, drinks, crowd, and music kept this party going until 10:30 p.m. in Kimberling City, Missouri.

Sunday morning at the Wilderness Road Festival. Would you believe the three of us never performed together until that morning? Three and one-half hours later, we finished playing all gospel music. Thanks go to Bob and Larry for helping make this a success.

RESCUE BAND

From Lampe, Missouri

A very good local country band. Shaun Campbell, the leader and founder of the group, may still be seen leading the band.

1st Annual Tomato Festival
Downtown Reeds Spring, Missouri

Saturday, August 2, 2014
10:00 A.M. to 6:00 P.M.

<u>ALL</u> PROCEEDS GO TO THE STUDENT "BACK PACK" PROGRAM

*Dunk Tank * Activities for Kids * Dutch Oven Demonstrations*
** Local Home-Grown Food and Home-Made Craft Vendors*
** Local Authors' Book Signings * Long-Time Residents' Historical Tales*

** Street Dance from 4:00 P.M to ???*

** Face Painting for Kids * Tomato Spoon Race * 3-Legged Race*
** Stick Horse Races * Much More*

10:00 A.M.	**Square Dancing**
11:15 – 1:15 A.M.	**Rescue Band**
1:30 P.M.	**Music by Tiffany**
2:00 P.M. – 2:45 P.M.	**Dave Warren**
3:00 P.M. – 4:00 P.M.	**Jim Wright**
4:00 P.M. - ???	**Highway 13 Band**

Schedule of entertainers of the first Tomato Festival. Great location, and the festival celebrates the large tomato industry, which once was the major industry in the Reeds Spring, Missouri, area.

Still singing and playing in my late fifties.

Left: Jim Wright. *Right*: Jim Brenan

Gary Lewis and I posing for the camera at the Dick Clark Theater, Branson, Missouri. What a great guy!

"Hey, let's twist again, everybody!" Here I am having a few laughs with Chubby Checker in Branson. Chubby had a big hit with "The Twist." Also, he released "The Hucklebuck."

Handsome, huh? That's me about in 1990.

10

Duck Walk

The 1950s introduced doo-wop singing styles, along with the crooners and torchlight singers of the 1940s and early 1950s, who would become, in 1964, just another page in musical history books.

The one influence that originated in the mid-1950s can still be heard in today's rock and roll and country music. That influence was the "lead guitar break." A black singer/songwriter guitarist would play his upscale, up-tempo songs with lyrics that told stories from girlfriends to auto racing to playing to the rhythm of the steam locomotives passing by. His music was fun, his music made you dance, his music wanted young boys to start buying electric guitars and becoming the next music superstar. His name? Chuck Berry, of course! Chuck managed to break into a predominately white industry because of his talent. His songs would go on to be played by the likes of the Beatles, Beach Boys, Rolling Stones, and ELO (Electric Light Orchestra).

His famous guitar licks would be copycatted by the best musicians around the world for decades and can still be heard on oldies radio stations today.

The first time I even appeared with Chuck was back in the late 1960s. Our band opened the show, followed by Status Quo ("Pictures of Matchstick Men"), the 1910 Fruitgum Company, and rounding out the show was Chuck Berry.

After the show, Chuck wanted to jam with the other musicians. Chuck was very critical of musicians who had no rhythm. He was also very vocal about telling someone if they "sucked."

By the end of our "star jam," Chuck had reduced a couple musicians to shreds. I was spared his wrath and actually was complimented on my musical ability.

That night, Chuck and I exchanged phone numbers and parted "respectful" of each other.

Chuck was truly an eccentric. Unfortunately, he had run-ins with drugs, alcohol, and the authorities. When he was sober, he would pack up his Gibson 335 and a small Fender amp in the back of a vintage Cadillac.

He lived in the St. Louis area and would drive to the Chicago area to find places to play. When he was in town, he would call me to see if I was available to make some music.

I can remember a story he once told me about pulling up to a bar in Niles, Michigan, one Saturday and asking the bartender (owner) if he could play.

The owner told him he had the night's band already lined up. Chuck proceeded to tell him he wanted to play right now! It was three thirty in the afternoon, and he told the gentleman that he was Chuck Berry. The bartender laughed and almost asked Chuck to leave—when Chuck said, "Let me bring my guitar in and play you a song, then you'll know who I am." The owner agreed. From the first note till the last one, sometime after 2:00 a.m., the place was rocking.

The owner and the few patrons at the bar called their friends to come see Chuck Berry, and boy, did they!

Another story that personally happened to me was a time Chuck came up on one of his Chicago trips. He and I were outside sitting in his Caddy, making our plans to jam. My mother had observed us sitting there for some time. I never really knew what my mother thought about my music. It was something we never really discussed.

Chuck and I agreed to meet and play later that night.

When I went back into the house, my mother asked, "Who was that black man you were talking to?"

"Oh, that was Chuck Berry," I replied.

While "ol' blue eyes" Frank Sinatra was my mom's favorite artist, she did know of Chuck Berry and wanted to hear how her son of mere garage band stardom came to be sitting in front of her house talking with a star of such magnitude.

Chuck would continue playing his songs well into his eighties at his club down in the St. Louis, Missouri, area with his son, who, by the way, was a very accomplished guitarist also.

I was so blessed to get to know Chuck in this world—may he "duckwalk" and play for those who preceded him.

11

My Kind of Town

Lots of great garage bands from Chicago made the big time. Local record companies like Dunwich Records and Columbia Records, locating a new recording facility in the west suburbs, brought many opportunities.

Dunwich had the Shadows of Knight and one of my all-time favorites, Saturday's Children, under contract. They were four guys from Northwest Indiana who could play, write songs, and handle vocals extremely well. "Leave That Baby Alone," "You Won't Leave Me Alone," and "Born on Saturday" were their best writings, and could they play the Beatles.

Columbia, on the other hand, had the Buckinghams and my all-time favorite band from Chicago—the Cryan' Shames. These guys could sing harmony like no one else. The Shames, as we called them, released the Drifters' 1963 hit "Up on the Roof." The Cryan' Shames made that song their own and had harmony that I did not know a group of voices could manufacture. They had four other hit songs and, onstage, would do the Animals and the Beatles. One of my favorite Beatles songs was "If I Needed Someone." Wow!

Another group Columbia signed was a group of Chicago music conservatory students named CTA, or the Chicago Transit Authority, after Chicago's mass transit system.

We were playing in a well-established three-story nightclub in Chicago one night. Jay, our equipment manager, went up to the third floor to see who the second band was that was playing that night. We were playing on the second floor, where the host band would play, and downstairs was a meet-and-greet bar.

After our first set, Jay came running over to us, saying, "You gotta see these guys on the third floor."

So we went. There that evening was CTA, and what a great sound with strong lead vocals, rock rhythms, jazz rhythms, blues rhythms, and horns. These guys harmonized their instruments—wow!

Pete Cetera from the band would go on to write songs and even write and perform a movie theme for Hollywood.

The same year, 1967, when we saw them, they had just released their first album, a two-record set on Columbia with songs like "Does Anybody Know What Time It Is?" and "Color My World."

The City of Chicago got really "hinky" over the use of the name CTA and lawyered up to have them change their name. The new name, Chicago, has lasted more than fifty years now.

A little-known record company called Vee-Jay was actually the first record company to release an album by the Beatles titled *Introducing the Beatles*, along with two 45s from the album. The records made so much for the little company that they moved from Gary to Chicago and would go on to record several local and name artists, including the Four Seasons.

Between the Eighteenth and Twenty-Second Streets on Michigan Avenue, you could find Record Row. Agents, recording studios, and record pressing companies could all be found there. Chuck Berry would come up to Chicago to record at Chess Studios. All of the major and private labels were made in this small little world within the confines of the City by the Lake, Chicago.

From being in "My Kind of Town" to "Cruisin' on LSD" (that's Lake Shore Drive, of course!), the city was a place to play and grow a career.

The West Coast was really the place to be to launch rock 'n' roll stardom with such greats as the Jefferson Airplane, Strawberry Alarm Clock, Grateful Dead, Sugarloaf, Iron Butterfly, and so many, many more big names.

I personally had no desire to go west as I felt there was plenty of opportunity right there in Chicago.

One of the main drawbacks of playing in the Greater Chicago area was labor unions. There were labor unions everywhere; why, you even had to join a union just to be a street and sanitation worker in Chicago.

There wasn't any difference with musicians either. Musicians were expected to carry a Musicians Guild card, and bars and other venues were expected to pay union wages.

The Musicians Guild would go so far as to check musicians for their union cards and ask to see owners' books that they were paying set wages. Quite frankly, I thought the union was quite "silly." They were never going to enforce everyone. They may have tried flexing their muscles on occasion, but there were just too many bands and too many places to play.

I can remember playing one afternoon in a battle of the bands competition held in one of the Chicago south suburbs' high school gym. We had just finished our performance when, only moments later, we stopped two sixteen-year-old boys from running up on stage.

A man from the local union hall bought the boys beer in exchange for them going up on stage and smashing our drums and amplifiers. Luckily, we saw them as they made their approach. We had heard this had happened a couple other times at high school dances, parties, etc.

As we interrogated the boys while waiting for the police, they described a union official I knew well.

On Monday afternoon after school, I went to the musicians' hall and paid the gentleman a visit. Needless to say, by the time our conversation was finished, I was most positive he wouldn't be doing any more dirty tricks.

I just reminded him of several laws he had broken, and although he was elderly, I didn't think he wanted to explain to his wife why he was sitting in jail and not having dinner with his family.

Back then, the Guild was secretly mob-run. Even the mob wouldn't do a thing to help him if he had gone off to jail.

The union was set up supposedly to find musicians work. From talking with other musicians, this rarely happened. I figured that the dues collected by the union went to support Democratic candidates in election races.

So much for the Windy City by the Lake.

12

One Hundred Sixty Miles of Gold

Chicagoland basically included every city and town from Milwaukee, Wisconsin, through Chicago, Illinois, on to Gary, Indiana, and winding up at the South Bend, Indiana, and Niles, Michigan, area.

There were lots of great places to play, like street dances, bowling alleys, resorts, restaurants, outdoor music theaters, drive-in movie theaters, and more.

South Bend, Indiana, was home to a band that never saw the oceans, never surfed, yet still has the number 1 surfing song of all time, "California Sun." The group was the Rivieras, and that one hit propelled them past the Beach Boys, Safaris, and the Astronauts for kings of "surfdom." The Rivieras can still be seen playing in the South Bend area.

Just up the road on Highway 35 was Niles, Michigan. Ted Nugent and the Amboy Dukes could be seen playing in that area. Ted is an avid hunter today.

Booker T. & the M.G.'s were from Niles also. Green Onions has been adopted by many car clubs as one of the greatest "cruisin" songs of all time. It's my favorite instrumental, for sure.

A lesser-known car song from Munster, Indiana, was "Car Hop" by the Exports on King Records. This song, while not selling many records, has slowly worked into the car music "cultdom."

The Mason Profit Band had five albums and stayed together for six years without a big hit. "Two Hangmen" only had some mild airplay. The group consisted of the Talbot Brothers and three other members based out of Munster, Indiana, too. John Talbot has been a Catholic monk for many years and lives in the Eureka Springs, Arkansas, area.

While all of these "garage bands" were breaking out, hundreds would fail.

Growing up in a predominately Polish neighborhood, my friends were trading accordions valued over $1,000 or more for $50 credit toward a guitar and amplifier, drums, or even portable organs.

Yet the bands kept coming: The Jaguars from Hammond, Indiana, and Calumet City, Illinois; the Basooties from Gary, Indiana; the Squires from Hammond's north side; the Mystics from Munster; the Critters from Munster, American Breed ("Bend Me, Shape Me"); and so many others like these who had steady local work and in some cases had a local Top 500 record.

One of the bands that stuck out in my mind was the Ides of March. Jim Peterik would go on to write the *Rocky* movie theme "Eye of the Tiger" while he was in a band called Survivor. He also was in the group 38 Special.

The Ides, as the DJs would call them, was in a battle of the bands competition against us. We finished first, and they finished second in that competition. The Ides' big hit was "Vehicle"; however, another favorite of mine by them was "L.A. Goodbye."

Oscar and the Majestics was a band from Gary, Indiana. The unique thing about this group was that a nameplate was attached to the necks of their guitars to keep the audience from seeing what chords they were playing. This was a totally absurd excuse to other musicians as to why the diversion, but that was Oscar. Oscar also took the McCoys' "Hang on Sloopy" and released a 45 single called "Come on Willie." Gee, I wonder how that went? WLTH Radio Gary played it some while the Majestics played it ad nauseam to the crowds.

The McCoys, while not a garage band from the area, came from Ohio. "Come On, Let's Go" and "Hang on Sloopy" were the only 45 releases I know of. Rick Derringer was the lead guitar and lead vocalist. Yes, it's the same Rick Derringer who would release the 1970s hit "Rock and Roll, Hoochie Koo." Derringer is one to be included as one of the '70s best rock 'n' roll lead guitarists.

The Oak Ridge Boys are best known for having a hit with the song "Elvira." A little-known group out of Milwaukee, Wisconsin, actually had a release of "Elvira" years before the Oak Ridge Boys in 1969. The name of the band was the Skunks, and trust me, these guys did not stink! They were a three-piece group that did various music and excelled in doing Beatles songs. We opened for them one night and were really impressed with their sound.

As you can see, that 160 miles of Lake Michigan shoreline had a gold mine of garage bands.

13

Through the Looking Glass

I figure, this being chapter 13 and all, I'd get the *Glory Days* in perspective through 1971.

In June or so of 1968, another group would come knocking. They fashioned their name to a piece of construction equipment like the Buffalo Springfield ("For What It's Worth"), a California-based band.

This group called themselves Manitowoc (a crane manufacturer), and it consisted of a drummer and lead and rhythm guitarists. They were looking for a bass player. I knew every song they played and was hired on the spot. I liked this group, and things started rolling in our favor when the two words I dreaded most came up after about six months—those words were Led Zeppelin. Jimmy Page of Yardbirds fame had this new band. Their music was all over the airwaves, and the others in our band thought we should drop songs to play Zeppelin. I was mortified. We were dropping Crosby, Stills, Nash & Young songs and others of the day for Led Zeppelin. I asked the guys if they were positive about their decision. They agreed they were, and I packed up and left.

Guess what? I fell back on folk music, and Mark, the agent, kept finding me fill-in jobs playing bass, guitar, drums, etc.

In January of 1969, I started picking up players to join "my" new band. I personally hand-picked each player. We played from 1969 through 1971. There were three guitarists and a bass guitar. I was playing second guitar at the time, playing leads and fill-ins. Our biggest problem was keeping a drummer. The drummers of the day wanted to play—you guessed it—Led Zeppelin.

It was three long years, and Mark, the agent, was getting me more backup work.

Occasionally, the band would go on short hiatus so I could rub shoulders with the stars.

By the end of 1971, I knew I was sick. My voice was almost gone from a throat infection I had since 1967. Eight doctors over four and a half years gave me antibiotics. It finally came to a climax when the father of a musician friend of mine who was a throat specialist gave me a birthday present in 1972 that I'll never forget. He took my adenoids, tonsils, and cancer from the top of my throat. Back then, everything was cancer. If they didn't know what something was, it was cancer. I was done for. I couldn't sing for almost six years directly due to the operation.

I had gotten married to my first wife in October of 1971, and I think she was relieved that my music career had come to the crossroads. So I had a job, a wife, and a home, but no voice. Early in 1974, I sold my guitars, amp—everything I owned except my microphone, which I still have, from the Jesters to that day.

One day in the spring of 1974, Mark, lead guitarist of the Jesters, called me. He and Ray, the drummer, wanted to put back some semblance of the Jesters. I agreed I'd like to, but I had sold everything. It was good to see them both, and I wanted the magic back. I could feel they wanted it too! We set up the equipment. I tried some vocals, to no avail. The magic had gone from all of us as hard as we tried to bring it back that night. We left Ray's house that night knowing that we would never see each other again as members of the band.

Mark and I talked some, and I saw him a few times. I could tell he was heartbroken, but I never knew until fifteen years later how hard Mark took not having the Jesters' magic in his life. He got married and worked at a local refinery, making good money.

The year 1989, I was a store manager for a local home center chain, and Ray happened into the store. I hadn't heard from Mark, and I asked Ray how he was doing. Ray got this real weird look on his face and gained his composure to tell me that Mark had loaded a .38 revolver and pulled the trigger. Mark so wanted music and playing in a band in his life that he took his own.

If there wasn't a hell of a band in the afterlife—there was now! God knows how I miss him.

By 1978, my voice started to come back. I did DJ work and started jamming again. My first wife was applying for a divorce, and I bought a new bass and amplifier.

I called Mark, the agent, to say I was back. His father had died, and the son was "modifying" their client list.

I kept DJing and filling in on bass where I could. DJ work kept me working.

A popular band in the area had a guy who I went to high school with and his brother. I went to see Jose's band one night at one of the popular night spots. I know Jose saw me, but he didn't come over to say hi. After two breaks and over two hours later, I caught him by the arm and spun him around.

Almost fifteen years earlier, I gave Jose his first bass lesson. If it had not been for that lesson, he would never have become the bassist he turned out to be. He became good, very good.

He said hello, and it was he who admitted that lesson got him started in music, and he thanked me right there on the spot. I thanked him for acknowledging my part in initiating his career.

P.S. His brother was one fine drummer, which I can't take credit for!

14

Rebirth

My job was taking me hither and yon, and in the late spring of 1981, I wound up in New Orleans. I had family there, and I wound up playing bass for a heavy metal band! Yes, a "metal" band in New Orleans! New Orleans was the home of jazz, not heavy metal.

We tried for three months to find a lead singer, to no avail. I didn't like New Orleans, and I left. I went back to Indiana and stayed with friends. I couldn't find a bass job anywhere.

I met a lot of good people with some of the social organizations I belonged to. I would meet my second wife in a Methodist church. We have been married for over forty years.

During the years 1985 to 1986, I played in a country band, and I DJed off and on through the 1980s.

In 1992, I started back to acoustic music. I played at numerous festivals in Lake and Porter Counties in Indiana.

I did a lot of emceeing at events and supplied sound systems, etc., for various fests and events.

I even produced shows and hired the entertainers for them. I used a lot of popular local acts.

My wife officially retired from the Federal Government, and my physical health was declining. We then and there decided to retire. In 2004, we moved to the Branson, Missouri, area. It was never my intention to play in a Branson show, and good thing I didn't. While Branson has some talented people and a few quality musicians, for the most part, I have never seen so many substandard players with attitude in my life!

One fellow I auditioned for a band didn't even know where a C chord was on his guitar; and he played in Branson, Missouri, twelve shows a week. There were others—drummers—who couldn't play fast; some couldn't play slow, and one even couldn't play at all!

Other players were envious of my former background.

A local restaurant hired me to do two nights a week with a neighbor who played keys. Due to schedules, we started doing one night together and one night solo. Eventually, I was playing on Thursday, Friday, and Saturday nights, and he would play one night solo during the week.

After almost two years, we had an obnoxious, belligerent drunk who thought he owned the place. He didn't want me to perform because he didn't want to be "bothered," as he put it.

He managed to watch two full sets with his wife and relatives and sat through one-half of the third set before he wandered into the bar to get even drunker. While in the bar, he met the owner's mother and complained about my lack of respect to him by starting my show after he told me not to.

The owner's mom never liked having live music in the restaurant anyway, so this was a good way to get rid of us. By Monday, we were gone because this drunk "lied" about what really happened.

I cut a solo CD, *Many Hats*, representing music that had been part of my life for so long. I even wrote three new songs for the album. The engineer recorded it in digital sound, and I wanted analog sound. Being the new engineer on the block with all the latest equipment, he thought digital would be best. It would take about eight years later, but he apologized and agreed I had been right. A couple of engineers in Branson showed him the error of his ways!

A friend of mine who managed a local restaurant called me wondering if I would be willing to start up a band with some other local musicians. I told him I would take a look.

The group came together and consisted of male and female singers, keyboards, guitar, drums, and I was on bass. We added a sax player six months later.

The group was getting a lot of work, and while we sounded great, the band had its problems. After almost two years, it was the only band I ever played in that voted me off the island. By this time, I had planned to leave after a county fair job we had scheduled in a couple of weeks. I knew the songs just "too well," background vocals, and the few lead vocals I did had been cut because the keyboard player was jealous of the audience's response to "my songs." Heck, the band couldn't lose an ego-driven keyboard player for an "award winner with better credentials" bass player, so off I went. I was more relieved than anyone will ever know.

The problem with most musicians? They generally are insecure. For example, *American Idol* parades thousands of kids through their auditions around the country to accumulate people who have talent and also show the ones with no talent, bad attitudes, or are socially dysfunctional.

Personally, these types of shows do a disservice to future applicants by showing them that even though one might have (truly) no talent, a bad attitude, or a social disorder, they don't stand a snowball's chance in hell of winning—they do have a chance of being on camera. The problem, as I see it, is the applicant still doesn't realize they don't have talent, a bad attitude; and the socially insecure go home feeling that the world has let them down again when they are rejected.

Luckily, I acquired talent and a good attitude, and I never once worried about insecurities when it came to me and my music.

15

And Justice for All

So far, I have spoken of some of the cast of characters whom I have met along my musical journey.

Remember Willie, my first lead player? After he left, he took a song I created, and his new band used it on the flip side of a 45 that came out. I think it sold 117 copies if I remember right.

Besides that, one of the members of his band had a bad habit of bad-mouthing the Jesters. We tried time and time again to offer a challenge to them, but time after time, they would run from the challenge.

On one special occasion, my school was having the Lettermen's Club dance. I already knew that Willie's band was hired for the job.

I went to the teacher in charge of the dance, Mr. Pape, and asked, "Who's playing for the dance?"

Mr. Pape didn't know I knew, so when he told me who it was, I said I had a band that needed a little exposure. Pape told me we could play for their breaks if that was okay.

I said, "You bet! We'll see you Friday afternoon."

The guys got excited. Finally, we manipulated our way in a heads-up, toe-to-toe match-up. It was like Christmas coming early. We got to the civic center early and set up. We had just finished setting up around 5:45 p.m. when I heard the voices of Willie and the others in the building.

They walked straight into the building, and I could hear at least one exclaim, "Hey, there's another band set up. Who are they?"

Mr. Pape had been in the room with us and walked out to greet them. The boys were all over him, wanting to know who else was playing. He told them he didn't know our name, and he probably wasn't lying. Pape wasn't big on details like names and such.

Well, the boys were stewing and pouting and whining enough, so I decided to step out in the hallway. The boys saw me, and the one who had been bad-mouthing us so much told Pape that they refused to play. Pape informed them that they could leave if they liked, but he had a band for the evening, so it didn't really matter.

To make a long story short, the boys did stay to take their lumps that evening. They let us play two forty-five-minute sets and go first—*big mistake*! We opened our first song with the Strawberry Alarm Clock's "Incense and Peppermints" and never stopped playing one big Top 40 hit after another.

As our first set ended, I introduced Willie's band, and the crowd jeered and booed! Willie and the boys bucked up and started their set, knowing their asses had just been handed to them.

Willie would go on to join a band from California a few years later. They had a couple of number 1 hits in Japan for two years but no success here at home. He would also find the drug culture and pay for this experience health-wise.

The following Monday, after defeating Willie's band, a fellow classmate, who was known for being the party animal when his folks were out of town, was by my side at my locker.

"Hey, Jim, old buddy, your band is great!"

This is the same guy who hadn't spoken to me the first two years of school. He wanted something. Well, he wanted our band to play at one of his soirees. I told him our rate was $187 per man and that we would be glad to play!

Needless to say, to this day, I still haven't spoken to him!

16

A "Diamond" Opportunity

In the late '60s, I received a call from a garage band from the east side of Hammond. They needed a lead guitarist to help them with some upcoming jobs and a contest they had entered. I told the fellow who called that I wasn't a lead player. I went down to meet them, and actually, I knew many of the songs they did on lead.

McCormick Place in Chicago, where a lot of bands played, had burned down; and the old Navy Pier and Ballroom had been cleaned up and put into service.

This band won a spot to compete for cash, instruments, and a recording contract. So we learned enough songs to show up and fall on our faces. We sucked!

Neil was performing at the ballroom and was walking around with who else but Agent Mark! Mark saw me, and I don't know which of us, him or me, were trying to hold back the pain of this moment.

Mark must have done some quick talking to Neil as they walked away.

As I remember, some months went by when I had just got home from work, and Mark was on the phone. He asked if I knew where a certain theater was in Chicago on the south side of the Loop. I said that I did, and he said, "Be here as soon as possible," and he hung up.

It was rush hour in Chicago, and trust me, no one was doing "as soon as possible" at that time of day. As I drove to the theater, I wondered what surprise Mark had for me. His call was different this time in that he would not tell me what I was doing. I pulled up to the theater, and Mark and a valet came out to meet me. The valet parked my car for me, and Mark and I walked into the lobby, only to behold Neil standing in anticipation of meeting me—ME? We shook hands, passed pleasantries, and then he asked me if I knew any of his songs. I told him I had his *Gold* album, which had every single he had out at the time. I mentioned I could play all but one of his eleven songs on the album. He seemed somewhat relieved, and off we went to do a run-through. I also knew some of the other songs he was doing in addition to the eleven off the album.

I found out that the run-through was not only my audition, but in a little over an hour, I would take the stage with Neil and his band. I even got to do some background vocals—wow!

I would be filling in for a few weeks for a band member who was out on personal leave.

Fortunately, I had a good boss, vacation time, and a crappy job, so I could do what I liked playing music with the likes of many different artists.

I was a mechanic out in the steel mills, and I trained or orientated all new mechanics. Nobody wants the new guys yet—that was my job, in addition to fixing things.

My boss knew I liked music and hated work. He knew I would leave someday, but he didn't want to lose me until that day came. With his blessing, I went, at least for the moment, to fulfill another chapter in my music resume.

The weeks passed, and there I was, back at work and working with my regular group again.

I stopped by the local music store to see what was new while I had been on tour with Neil when my buddy Dan, the bassist, came up to me.

He wanted to shake my hand and thank me for not being in town and on the road with Neil as he had auditioned for the Zombies ("Tell Her No" and "She's Not There") and got the job going on tour with the Zombies on their "Time of the Season" tour. The Zombies hadn't had an international hit since 1964 and was embarking on a new tour. Dan had landed a two-year guaranteed contract. I bid him good luck, and we parted for the last time, as we would never see each other again.

I miss Dan and our friendly rivalry—a good bassist and a good friend.

17

For God's Sake

Three months after my throat surgery, a newly found friend, Carlton, invited me one night for a beer and hot dogs at our nearest Lum's Restaurant.

He was looking for musicians to perform a gospel program entitled *He's Alive*. At that time, *Jesus Christ Superstar* was big, along with *Godspell*, another hip revival stage musical. He asked me to take a tape home and listen to it with no "strings" attached. I took it home, and at first, I was just going to give it back—but then I chose to listen to it. I called him three days later, and we got together to talk about the particulars. The fact that sealed the deal was that I didn't have to sing at all and only play background instruments. Off and on, we played various churches, etc., doing *He's Alive*. I played guitar on a few songs and drums on everything else. The choir did the singing. I just played—thank you, God!

It would be over forty years later that I would be asked to do a gospel program.

A local festival called me to put on a gospel program. The only problem was it was only three days before the event. I didn't do but a handful of gospel, and they needed a two-hour show. Come Sunday morning, some musician friends of mine and I put on an acoustic gospel program. From the first song to the last, we were a success. A crowd stayed all morning to hear our performance of favorite gospel songs.

Everyone liked the show so well that a week later, I got a small check from the festival committee in appreciation of my efforts.

I performed at a couple of local churches and a nursing home, doing a mix of gospel and contemporary music.

In 2012, I put a gospel program together for a festival in Reeds Spring, Missouri. It was larger than the Branson Gospel Fest and the world-famous Silver Dollar City Gospel Fest. We had groups from seven different states come in, plus the president of gospel music in Nashville, Tennessee. We also had artists who just "showed up" to be a part of the event.

It went so well that these blessed entertainers performed in the cold and the rain of early October, and a loyal crowd sat, stood, clapped, and praised Jesus's name right along with them. Before the event was over, they wanted to come back next year. Unfortunately, due to politics, next year never came.

At least a reunion of these performers is inevitable. It just might be on "the other side," if you know what I mean.

18

Names and Numbers

Opening for big-name acts was an act of skill and futility. While we were supposed to open for the same show for several concerts at a time, sometimes the schedule would change.

One such instance I can remember was when we were supposed to open for the First Edition. "Something's Burning" was a huge hit for them, and they were kicked to a different tour due to their success. Their replacement was another girl-guy band, the We Five, and they had a monster hit, "You Were on My Mind."

We opened for all kinds of rock /pop / Top 40 stars. I think most of the stars either got it together or got out of the business. Playing the same songs on the road seven days a week, playing up to three shows a day, and riding on a bus did take a toll on a lot of performers.

Speed and booze seemed to be some of the stars' traveling companions. One black group that was one of the pioneers in bridging the gap from all-black to all-white music stations has a member whom the band was named after. We appeared ten times with them. The namesake of the group has a drug and alcohol problem. Only once did I ever see him play with any sobriety at all. Twice, they had to hold him steady and upright, and seven times he was a no-show. Sometimes, the band would play without him just to fulfill a contractual obligation.

The Lovin' Spoonful was a terrific band and played such fun music. They lasted only about two years with the original members as drugs had crept into their lives and tore the band apart. John Sebastian would go on to write and perform the theme song for the television show *Welcome Back Kotter*. Drugs would take the lead player's life. The bassist and drummer perform at 1960s reunion shows, fairs, and festivals.

We got a chance to open for the Turtles and the Animals at a local civic auditorium in town. It was our first time playing in front of either group. The Turtles had their two front men, Flo (Phlorescent Leech) and Eddie. They were both Jewish and would put on this comedy "schtick" between songs. Most of their "schtick" wasn't funny, and they would go on and on at times when they should have gone to the next song. Their vocal capability far surpassed their comedy quotient—lots of great songs and good memories.

We showed up that night at the auditorium and realized we had forgotten a much-needed piece of equipment. I called my mom, and she brought it to us. She entered the building, and in moments, she had been pushed out of the way by none other than Eric Burden of the Animals and the rest of the band.

My mom yelled, "You can say 'Excuse me,'" and Eric gave her the finger and went into a room with the band down the hall. She walked into the room and asked Eric to apologize for his rudeness, and needless to say, Eric uttered a profanity. My mom turned to the door, grabbed a local police officer she knew, and told him he should lock Eric up for drunk, disorderly, and assault.

Miraculously, Eric apologized to her, and she said to him, "A night in jail might do you good, son." My mom waited a few moments longer just to see some more sweat roll off the Animals' band and management's foreheads.

I hear she got him to get on his knees to make the apology.

We did get our equipment, the show went on, and my mom later asked me what the name of that "lil' puke" was.

"Animals, huh? That's a good name for their band!"

One thing was certain: I was lucky to meet various artists of the 1960s pop music culture.

Lots of band members would leave folk music groups, such as the New Christy Minstrels, for a shot at the big time, like Kenny Rogers of the First Edition and Jim Roger McGuinn, lead guitar of the Byrds.

To this day, I do several Byrds' hits when I perform. They played a lot of electric folk music and songs amped up to the Byrds' style from Bob Dylan.

Some band members were fortunate to find even better jobs after their band broke up. Unfortunately, drugs and lifestyle brought many musicians to their knees, and in some cases, stars would accidentally drug overdose.

I was fortunate that the drug scene never even aroused my curiosity. Most of the guys I played with, while I knew them, weren't into the drug scene either.

The 1960s and early 1970s were a good time, a crazy time, and such an emotional time for everyone.

By the mid-1970s, the garage band era was over, and some of the previous hitmakers of the 1960s got chances to go on to even more notoriety in the 1970s.

The guitars and amps were being made better, sound quality drastically improved, and keyboards became sophisticated computers.

Times had changed, and the music had changed. However, the one constant was musicians. Wherever they may be and whoever they may be, they were still making music.

19

More Name-Droppin'

I have written about some of the many names already, and this chapter is dedicated to even more name-dropping.

Bubble gum music was big, it seemed, long about 1967. The 1910 Fruitgum Company had hits with "Yummy, Yummy, Yummy" and "Chewy Chewy." In 1968, I was able to open for this band. They would start each show with all of their hits—like all five of them. They would then spend the rest of their stage time being one of the best blues bands you will ever hear! Yes, blues band!

I also got to open for Frank Zappa, and yes, he was "real." I remember Frank starting about ten minutes late, and during that whole time, Frank and the band were tuning their instruments. Frank turned to a microphone and said, "We gotta tune, or we might sound like shit." He turned and walked away, then abruptly turned back to the microphone and added, "Not that we won't sound like shit anyway." The audience roared with laughter.

By my final year, 1971, before my surgery, I got to open for Styx, REO Speed Wagon, the Mauds, Aorta, New Colony Six, Michael and the Messengers, the Buckinghams, Rapid Transit, and the Flock, just to name a few.

My favorite Chicago group? All of them, of course!

There also were the superstars like the Who, the Kinks, Peter and Gordon, the Animals, the Turtles, the Hollies, Sly and the Family

Stone, the Association, Green Lyte Sunday, and the Mindbenders less Wayne Fontana.

I also got to jam with Edgar Winter in Mississippi in the lobby of a hotel on one absolutely dreadful rainy night in the late 1970s. Just as his bus was pulling into the driveway, there was a scream from one of the stewardesses (flight attendant), who was part of a flight crew that was grounded due to the storm. Her room was next to mine, as I found out, and her scream came from the fact that there were bullet holes from a previous guest's stay in that room. The bullet holes were part of the ambiance of this hotel's superlative accommodations that I don't think she cared for.

Anyway, we jammed for a while into the night—what a treat being able to jam with Edgar.

Sometimes in my travels with my job, I would get a chance to play with the house band or perform folk music onstage at the hotels where I stayed.

I was at the Eldorado, Arkansas, Holiday Inn and struck up a conversation with a young salesman from Memphis. We shared our life histories, and I mentioned that I played guitar. At some point, he asked the band if I could sit in. At the start of the second set, the band asked me to come up on stage. The salesman urged me, and up I went. The problem with the stage was it had a three-foot square hole about eighteen inches deep right on the side I was standing. I called out, "'Johnny B. Goode' in A," and we took off. I just started singing when I stepped back. Next thing I knew, an amplifier, guitar, and I were lying in a heap together. Everyone in the place died laughing, even me.

I got up, and we started again (that's what a professional does), and without further incident, I finished the song. I don't remember how many more songs I did, but the band offered me a job for $110 a week, meals, and lodging. Needless to say, I thanked them for the offer and went back to where my salesman friend had a drink already ordered for me. We talked a bit more and wished each other safe travel.

I mentioned how several times my music has been challenged. One night, a young man approached me as Neil Diamond was his favorite artist, and he couldn't believe I worked with him. He asked me twenty-two questions about Neil, not because he wanted to know about him, but instead, he was "testing" me. After answering his questions, he now wanted to be a "friend" of the "friend," if you know what I mean.

Around the same time, I was working as a store manager for a Chicago home improvement company. Our flooring department manager couldn't believe my past either, and he came up with my latest challenge. His buddy had a blues band that was playing at a club on the southeast side of Chicago. He invited me to come hear them, and I accepted. The band played their first set. After their break, I would play for almost four hours until I said, "I gotta get home." They finished their last set without me. On Monday, our floor manager was all smiles, handshakes, apologetic (for not believing me), and complimentary of my playing that night.

Today, I still do some acoustic gigs, and I still put on entertainment for local festivals and organizations. There are still those who are a "doubting Thomas," jealous critics, and, of course, fans.

Looking back, I am most grateful for over fifty-five years of doing what I like best—music.

In 1972, as I lay recovering from my throat surgery, my mother's words expressed that maybe I should get a real occupation and leave my music to the past. I thought at first she was right. I'm glad I never completely gave up the one constant that was in my life—my music. Thus, this must be the *Glory Days*.

About the Author

Jim grew up in Northwest Indiana, where he played music in and around the nearby Chicago area. For the past twenty years, he has lived in Southern Missouri with his wife of forty-two years. He has been active in local civic organizations and has taught evening classes at a local adult education center. Jim has been known to put on music shows for small town festivals and play solo for meetings and luncheon venues for business and social groups. He and his wife have dabbled in antiques and participated in area model train shows. Jim has been interested in collecting model trains since age six. To this day, he still has substantial collections of toy trains, collector albums, and 45s. Jim also likes to acquire rare records of Chicago groups from the 1960s and 1970s.

www.ingramcontent.com/pod-product-compliance
Lightning Source LLC
Chambersburg PA
CBHW041650150726
48005CB00013BA/1602